T0040645

COVER YOUR ASSETS

The Teens' Guide to Protecting Their Money and Their Stuff

by KARA McGUIRE

COMPASS POINT BOOKS

a capstone imprint

Compass Point Books are published by Capstone,
1710 Roe Crest Drive, North Mankato, Minnesota 56003
www.capstonepub.com

Editorial Credits
Angie Kaelberer and Catherine Neitge, editors; Ted Williams, designer;
Eric Gohl, media researcher; Laura Manthe, production specialist

Image Credits
Alamy: EPA European Pressphoto Agency b.v., 27; Getty Images: Tim Boyles,
8–9; iStockphotos: tomeng, 26; Shutterstock: asife, 40, bikeriderlondon, 18–19,
Blazej Lyjak, 42–43, blue67design, 56, Carlos Amarillo, 23, Eric Isselee, 36–37,
Filipe Frazao, 50–51, IhorZigor, 33, kovacsf, 28, Lisa S., cover, Little Whale,
48–49, Masson, 34–35, Mesut Dogan, 53, michaeljung, 14, 30–31, Monkey
Business Images, 10, My Good Images, 7, Orhan Cam, 54, Pavel L Photo and
Video, 4–5, ponsulak, 46–47, Rido, 13, Room27, 25 (background), Samuel
Borges Photography, 21, Stephen VanHorn, 45, Tristan Scholze, 58–59, Valua
Vitaly, 1, zimmytws, 38, Zorandim, 16

Design Elements: Shutterstock

Library of Congress Cataloging-in-Publication Data
McGuire, Kara.
  Cover your assets : the teens' guide to protecting their money and their stuff
/ by Kara McGuire.
    pages cm.—(Compass point books. Financial literacy)
  Includes bibliographical references and index.
  ISBN 978-0-7565-4921-3 (library binding)
  ISBN 978-0-7565-4930-5 (paperback)
  ISBN 978-0-7565-4938-1 (eBook PDF)
  1. Insurance—Juvenile literature. 2. Finance, Personal—Juvenile literature.
3. Teenagers—Finance, Personal—Juvenile literature. I. Title.
  HG8052.5.M34 2015
  368.00835—dc23   2014003568

TABLE OF CONTENTS

PROTECT YOURSELF!

Do you remember the first time you lost something that was important to you? Say you were 5 and took your brand new change purse or pencil case to school. At the end of the school day, it was nowhere to be found. You can probably still remember the feeling of loss that enveloped you when you realized that your prized possession was gone forever. Some losses can't be prevented. But there are ways to prepare for others. Being able to handle loss when it happens is one reason to plan and save. Another way to protect yourself is to buy insurance. Some types of policies make more sense for a young adult to have than others. Not sure how they work? There are several types of policies, but they all work to protect you or your possessions. And what about protecting your identity? Identity theft can be worse than a car theft or a break-in at your house. There are several steps you can take to protect yourself from becoming an identity theft victim.

CHAPTER ONE

THE BASICS:
RISK AND INSURANCE

Without risk, there would be no need for insurance. Risk—the possibility that something bad will happen—is all around us, all the time.

It is impossible to erase risk from our lives. But there are ways to deal with it. You can:

- *Steer clear of risk.* **Some risks can be avoided altogether. For example, you can choose never to smoke cigarettes or accept a ride from someone who has been drinking alcohol.**

- *Reduce risk.* **It is possible to reduce the risk that bad things will happen. For example, you can wear a helmet when riding your bike, or leave lights on a timer each time you go on vacation to deter burglars.**

- *Share risk.* **This is what you are doing when you purchase insurance. You are spreading out the risk so if something bad happens, you won't have to handle it all by yourself.**

Do you remember a time when you were taking a risk that made you feel uncomfortable? Maybe your palms were sweaty or you were sick to your stomach. Maybe you couldn't concentrate on anything else or found your mind racing to the worst-case scenario.

Various people have various risk tolerance. If you were about to cross the Grand Canyon on a high wire, you'd probably have all of the symptoms described above and then some. But daredevil Nik Wallenda, who has been walking on a wire since he was 2, would assess the risk of walking on a steel cable high above the Colorado River differently. In June 2013 he took just less than 23 minutes to successfully complete this incredibly risky stunt.

Nik Wallenda crossing the Grand Canyon

Risk tolerance also varies by situation. You may not be able to walk a high wire, but you might be comfortable with the risk of injury when playing your favorite sport or the risk of losing money in the stock market.

THE YOUNG AND THE RISKY

Scientists have learned that the frontal cortex—the part of the brain in charge of impulse control, judging risk, and making decisions—isn't fully developed until a person is 25 years old. This is one reason car insurance costs more for teens and young adults. Unmarried men who are younger than 25 pay the most for car insurance.

WHAT IS INSURANCE?

Insurance is designed to protect you and your finances when something unfortunate and unexpected takes place. Its purpose is to mitigate (lessen) the risk. When you buy an insurance policy, you're basically buying a contract that says if certain adverse things happen, the insurance company will cover agreed-upon costs for you, the policyholder. The contract explains what the insurance will and won't cover. For example, health insurance won't cover every medical procedure, and car insurance won't cover every breakdown. Yet these policies will cover the major mishaps that could wipe out your savings or your parents' or guardians' savings.

There are many types of insurance—too many to list here. But the basic types of insurance cover people, such as yourself or your family, or property, including your car, home, or personal belongings. Life, disability, and health insurance fall in the first group. Car insurance and homeowners or renters insurance fall in the second. You can even purchase small insurance policies for your smartphone or to refund your airfare in case you have to cancel a vacation.

Insurance policies vary in price, based on many factors. For example, living in an area with a higher crime rate will result in more expensive renters insurance. Driving a sports car or simply being a new driver will cause higher car insurance rates. Smoking cigarettes will lead to costlier life insurance.

No one likes to think of paying for something he or she will never use. Some risks are too costly to cover on your own. When choosing whether to buy insurance, you need to ask yourself if you could afford to pay the costs of a health or property emergency up front. If the answer is no, you'd better buy insurance. If the answer is yes, then you need to set enough money aside in a savings account to cover any potential losses. Otherwise a loss could blindside you.

Deciding whether to purchase insurance is up to you—to some degree. For example, you must have health insurance or face a penalty. And you are required to have auto insurance in most states, but no one will force you to buy insurance for your smartphone.

WHERE TO BUY

You can buy insurance online, through a site that collects information from multiple insurance companies to make it easier to compare policies and prices. Or you can buy directly from an insurer's website or mobile app. You also can buy insurance through an insurance agent, who will help determine the right policy for you and take care of the paperwork. Some agents are independent, meaning that they can sell policies from more than one insurance company. Others are captive agents, selling policies from only one company. You will have more choices with an independent agent. Insurance agents make their money through commissions earned from the company selling the policy.

shopping, you'll receive an estimated price called a quote for the type of policy you're considering, based on information you've given them about yourself and your insurance needs. If you choose to buy the insurance policy, your cost is called a premium.

If you ever need to use an insurance policy, known as making a claim, you will usually pay a deductible. This amount is what you are responsible to pay before the insurance company will make a payout. Deductibles vary in amount. Generally, the higher the deductible, the lower the premium. Always set aside enough money in a savings account to pay your deductible so that your deductible doesn't become debt.

PAYMENT OPTIONS

You'll usually have several options for paying your insurance premiums. You often have the choice to pay monthly, quarterly, or annually. Sometimes paying a lump sum instead of monthly payments will net you a decent discount. You can have the money automatically withdrawn from your bank account or be billed for the premium. If you receive health insurance through an employer, your premium will be deducted from your paycheck. Homeowners often automatically pay their house insurance along with their mortgage payment from what's called an escrow account.

If you forget to pay your premium or don't have the funds to cover it, most insurers will give you about 30 days to pay before canceling your policy. Letting your insurance policy lapse is a pain. If it's a life insurance policy, you may have to go through another health examination and could end up paying more for your policy.

If the policy is for auto insurance, the consequences are even more serious. A lapse of even one day could raise your rate once you buy a new policy, because uninsured drivers are considered higher risk. Not only that, but driving without at least liability insurance is illegal in every state but New Hampshire. And if you have a car loan, you are required to have insurance. If you don't buy your own policy, the lender will buy a policy for you at a very steep rate. In an extreme case, the lender might repossess your wheels.

If you take out a loan to buy a home, you'll also need insurance. Mortgage holders require homeowners to have insurance and will purchase extremely expensive insurance for the homeowner if the situation isn't corrected right away. For those with renters insurance, if your policy lapses and the rental unit experiences a fire or other disaster, you're out not only the cost of a policy you never used, but also the replacement cost of every one of your possessions.

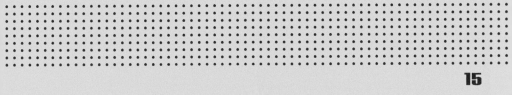

KNOW THE SCORE

Before an insurance company decides whether to offer you an insurance policy and at what premium, the company assesses how risky it will be to insure you. There are many ways that the insurance company will assess a potential customer's risk. It will look at past behavior—have you been in previous car accidents, do you lose a lot of items, or are you known to jump out of airplanes? It will take into consideration what you are insuring and where. For example, a sports car in a city with a high crime rate will typically cost a lot more to insure than a minivan in the suburbs.

An insurer will also look at your financial behavior, particularly how you handle credit. Insurers have found that a person's credit behavior can predict how likely it is for that person to have an insurance loss. Some states have restrictions on how credit-based insurance scores are used. But the bottom line is that the way you handle credit can affect other areas of your life, so it is important to use credit responsibly.

KEEPING AHEAD OF CHANGE

Life changes a lot when you're young. Think of all the scenarios. You might buy a car, move to a different state, switch jobs, or get married. Each time your life changes, you'll need to look at whether your insurance needs have changed as well.

Even in years when you don't have a major life event, it pays to reevaluate your policies. Premiums fluctuate based on market conditions and can go down. As you get older and exhibit responsible behavior such as paying your premium on time, you may be offered a lower premium. Check your policy and its premium every couple of years.

DO I REALLY NEED IT?

You might wonder if you really need to worry about insurance. After all, you're just a teen—you probably don't have much to protect. And some of the insurance policies your parents have will protect you as well. For example, federal law requires health care companies to allow young adults to stay on their parents' policy until they turn 26, even if they are married and financially independent.

If you're living at home, you can stay on your parents' car insurance as well, regardless of how old you are. Usually you can stay on your parents' policy when you're in college too, because your dorm room is not considered your permanent residence.

Sometimes your parents' homeowners insurance policy will also cover your belongings at college. Be sure to have them contact their agent or read the details of their policy. Otherwise you should find the money in your budget to buy a renters insurance policy, even in a dorm room. Bottom line, you should always have health insurance, disability insurance, renters or homeowners insurance, and auto insurance, whether it's your parents' policy or your own.

KEEPING IT SOCIAL

Social media can be a great way to keep in touch with the companies that have your business. The companies' Facebook pages and Twitter feeds can contain a lot of valuable and entertaining information. But you should be careful about the types of posts and photos you place on your social media pages. What you share via social media could be considered by insurance companies when evaluating your policy or examining a claim

CHAPTER TWO PROTECTING YOUR STUFF

Buying a car is a big deal. You have to save for a long time, research which car to buy, and find the right vehicle. Then the moment comes, and you get to slide behind the wheel. It's an exciting moment. But it's also a little nerve-wracking. What if something goes wrong? That's what insurance is for.

If an accident happens, car insurance can help pay for:

- *Damage to your car.*

- *Damage you cause in an accident.*

- *Medical bills for injuries from a car accident.*

- *Damage caused by a noninsured driver. Even though most states require car insurance, not every driver purchases it.*

Car insurance includes several components. Some are optional and some aren't. The requirements vary by state. Scrimping on insurance can be risky, and often adding a little more coverage doesn't cost that much more. An insurance agent or quick web search on insurance minimums in your state can help you start thinking about how much insurance to buy.

There are six parts to basic auto insurance:

- *Bodily injury liability pays for injuries you cause to someone else, whether you're driving your own car or someone else's with their permission.*

- *Personal injury protection pays for your injuries and the injuries of your passengers. It also helps cover lost wages in case you can't immediately return to work.*

- *Property damage liability pays for damage you cause to another person's car or property.*

- *Collision pays for damage to your car, whether it's a fender bender or a car-crushing crash, and regardless of whose fault it is. The insurance company will pay to get your car fixed, or give you a certain amount toward a new car if your old car is totaled.*

- *Comprehensive covers damage or loss of your vehicle that's not caused in a crash. For example, if a tree branch falls on your car, comprehensive kicks in. If your car is stolen, comprehensive pays. Older cars might need less or no comprehensive insurance. It depends on how much your car is worth and whether you have savings to pay for a new one if needed.*

- *Underinsured and uninsured coverage kicks in if you're involved in a hit-and-run accident or an accident involving an uninsured driver.*

Homeowners insurance covers the cost of rebuilding your house and replacing the belongings inside in the event of a fire or other disaster. Renters insurance covers the loss of personal property inside a rented home or apartment. Your parents' home insurance may cover your personal belongings, even if you are attending college and living away from home. If that's not the case, strongly consider a renters insurance policy. You may think you don't own much of value. But if you own a few electronic devices, a closetful of clothes, and a few pieces of furniture, odds are you couldn't afford to replace them all without wiping out most or all of your savings.

To gauge how much your possessions are worth, do a home inventory. You can walk around your bedroom, house, or apartment and write down your belongings, with an estimate of what amount they're worth. Taking a video and storing it in a safe-deposit box, the cloud, or other secure location is also a helpful way to inventory your stuff.

Remember that insurance isn't just for large items such as cars and TVs. For example, you can insure your smartphone or tablet. If you lose your smartphone, it's reasonable to consider buying another one with your savings or downgrading to a basic phone until you can afford a better one. It's also reasonable to pay $10 a month for insurance that will replace your phone if you drop it. What you decide depends on many factors, but mostly your risk tolerance.

Teen Inventory

Item	Replacement Value
TV	
Game System	
Computer	
Tablet	
Phone	
Bed	
Bureau/Dresser	
Desk	
Clothes	
Shoes	
Books	
Jewelry	

INSURING YOUR RIDE

Did you know that your car insurance rates depend in part on the car that you drive? Check out Insure.com's list of the top five least expensive and most expensive cars to insure. Is your dream car not on either list? The bottom line is that if it's sporty and imported, expect to pay far more.

The five most expensive cars to insure:

Rank	Make & model (all 2013)	Avg. annual premium
1	Nissan GT-R Track Edition	$ 3,169
2	BMW M6	$ 3,065
3	Mercedes-Benz CL550 4Matic AWD	$ 3,019
4	Mercedes-Benz SLS AMG GT	$ 2,986
5	Porsche Panamera Turbo S	$ 2,970

http://www.insure.com/car-insurance/most-expensive-cars-to-insure/

Jeep Wrangler Sport

Nissan GT-R Track Edition

The five least expensive cars to insure:

Rank	Make & model (all 2013)	Avg. annual premium
1	Jeep Wrangler Sport	$1,080
2	Honda Odyssey LX	$1,103
3	Jeep Patriot Sport	$1,104
4	Honda CR-V LX	$1,115
5	Jeep Compass Sport	$1,140

http://www.insure.com/car-insurance/least-expensive-cars-to-insure/

Where you live also affects your auto insurance premium. You can use carinsurance.com's "Nosy Neighbor" calculator to see how insurance rates fluctuate by ZIP code.

2014 STATE RANKINGS OF CAR INSURANCE RATES

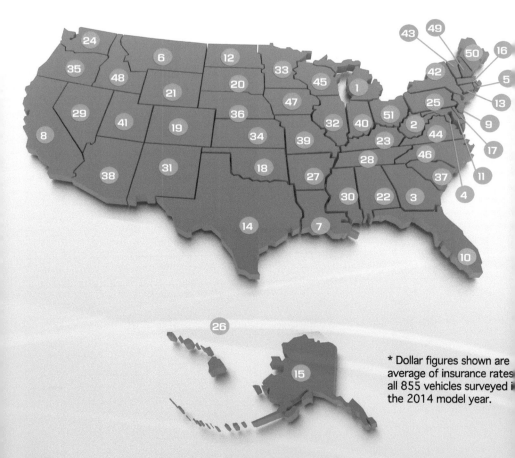

* Dollar figures shown are average of insurance rates all 855 vehicles surveyed i the 2014 model year.

Rank	State	Avg. annual premium*	Rank	State	Avg. annual premium*
1	Michigan	$ 2,551	26	Hawaii	$ 1,400
2	West Virginia	$ 2,518	27	Arkansas	$ 1,399
3	Georgia	$ 2,201	28	Tennessee	$ 1,397
4	Washington, D.C.	$ 2,127	29	Nevada	$ 1,388
5	Rhode Island	$ 2,020	30	Mississippi	$ 1,385
6	Montana	$ 2,013	31	New Mexico	$ 1,371
7	Louisiana	$ 1,971	32	Illinois	$ 1,370
8	California	$ 1,962	33	Minnesota	$ 1,360
9	New Jersey	$ 1,905	34	Kansas	$ 1,358
10	Florida	$ 1,830	35	Oregon	$ 1,333
11	Maryland	$ 1,810	36	Nebraska	$ 1,317
12	North Dakota	$ 1,710	37	South Carolina	$ 1,316
13	Connecticut	$ 1,638	38	Arizona	$ 1,222
14	Texas	$ 1,620	39	Missouri	$ 1,207
15	Alaska	$ 1,605	40	Indiana	$ 1,202
16	Massachusetts	$ 1,604	41	Utah	$ 1,192
17	Delaware	$ 1,580	42	New York	$ 1,173
18	Oklahoma	$ 1,568	43	Vermont	$ 1,149
19	Colorado	$ 1,558	44	Virginia	$ 1,114
20	South Dakota	$ 1,557	45	Wisconsin	$ 1,087
21	Wyoming	$ 1,541	46	North Carolina	$ 1,060
22	Alabama	$ 1,529	47	Iowa	$ 1,058
	National average	$ 1,503	48	Idaho	$ 1,053
23	Kentucky	$ 1,503	49	New Hampshire	$ 983
24	Washington	$ 1,499	50	Maine	$ 964
25	Pennsylvania	$ 1,440	51	Ohio	$ 926

Source: http://www.insure.com/car-insurance/car-insurance-rates.html

PREMIUM BEHAVIOR

Some insurance companies offer discounts for certain types of behavior. If, for example, you pay your premium all at once instead of monthly, you might receive a small discount. Other potential discount-worthy behavior includes:

- Getting good grades.

- Taking a defensive driving course.

- Having a car alarm.

- Purchasing multiple policies, such as home or auto insurance, from the same company.

- Allowing a car insurance company to record your behind-the-wheel behavior with a small device. Good behavior means a lower premium. This is called usage-based insurance.

Have you ever bought a TV, smartphone, or computer and had the salesperson lean in to share unsettling stories about the odds of your new gadget's breaking? Why would they do that? So they can explain that for a small fee, you'll be protected—either in the form of a new item or a free repair—if your new item goes kaput.

They're attempting to sell you a warranty. Typically, a warranty promises that if something goes wrong with an item because of a defect, the item will be repaired or replaced at no cost. A warranty is essentially a type of insurance—it's an agreement from the manufacturer that the customer will be compensated for problems in certain circumstances.

Most consumer purchases include a manufacturer's warranty for a certain period of time, such as 90 days to a year. Cars usually have warranties for a period of time or a certain number of miles, whichever comes first.

Warranties don't cover everything. They don't go into effect if the problem is your fault, or if it results from general wear and tear. For example, if you get in a fight with your brother and throw the remote through the new TV, a warranty wouldn't cover the damage. And if you've had the TV for 15 years and the picture starts to look fuzzy, chances are a manufacturer won't replace it. But if the picture on your brand-new TV isn't clear and sharp, the company will either offer to repair it or give you a new TV.

EXTENDED WARRANTIES

Basic warranties that come with products are free. But it's typical for a salesperson to try to sell you additional protection, especially on expensive items. These plans are called extended warranties.

In general, consumer experts say extended warranties don't make much sense. Often an extended warranty costs too much, duplicates the coverage that comes with the manufacturer's warranty, or fails to cover what is most likely to break. Instead of buying an extended warranty, consider setting aside the cost of the warranty in a savings account. That way you can replace or repair the item yourself. If it doesn't break, you have extra cash in the bank.

Like all money decisions, emotion can play a role in deciding whether to purchase an additional warranty. If a warranty gives you peace of mind, then it's OK to buy one. Just be sure to understand what's covered by reading the fine print.

FACT: If you buy an extended warranty and change your mind, you may be entitled to a partial or full refund within a certain period of time. Read the fine print to learn if your extended warranty has this feature.

CHAPTER THREE

PROTECTING YOURSELF

You've learned how to use insurance to protect some of your most important assets — your car, smartphone, and furniture. But there is one asset that cannot be replaced: YOU. Your ability to work. Your identity. Your life.

There are some tools for protection that may not even register on your radar screen. You probably figure that you're just a teen and life isn't complicated enough to have a will or life insurance. Let's see if that assumption is correct.

A will is a legal document that sets up what you'd like to happen to your property when you die. While most teens' financial lives are pretty uncomplicated, a will is a good idea if you feel strongly about which of your siblings would get your dirt bike or jewelry, or if you have a beloved pet that would need a new home. If you do have assets, either from saving or by inheriting money or property from a relative, having a will is even more important. A will is an absolute must if you have a partner or children. A will establishes guardianship—who will take care of your child if you die. You don't want to leave that decision up to the court system.

You can use legal websites or computer software to create a simple will. If you'd rather get professional help, start with your parents' or guardians' lawyer, if they have one. Some law firms also do free legal work for certain groups, including teens. Legal aid groups, which are made up of lawyers who volunteer their time to help low-income people with legal problems, are another option.

LIFE INSURANCE POLICY

Terms used in this Policy

The following describe your rights and obligations under this Policy.

We, us, our and the Company mean Life Insurance Company.

You and your means the Policy Owner named in the Policy Schedule.

Administrative rules means the rules and procedures we establish to facilitate the ___ on of ___ive ___

We may amend our administrative rules from time to time. Any changes we make to ___

alter any guarantee or benefit provided by this Policy.

Attained Age means a Life Insured's Insurance Age plus the number of ___ from th ___ licy Da ___

Policy Anniversary.

Beneficiary means the person or entity entitled to receive the Death Benefit when th ___ esignat ___

Class means a grouping of individuals satisfying underwriting criteria related to specified aspe ___

tobacco usage, family history and other personal history. Based on these criteria, a Life Insu ___

as either a Smoker or a Non-Smoker, and is either a Preferred or Standard Class. We dete ___

applicable to each Life Insured and use it to establish his or her Premium. It is specified in ___

8. When your insurance ends

If you're an average teen, the answer is no. Life insurance is designed to provide financially for your loved ones when you die. It's typically used to replace the income earned by the person who died and to cover large expenses such as the cost of college for the person's children.

Teens typically don't have children or large incomes to replace. If you do work and have a family, you might consider a term life insurance policy. It covers the policyholder for a certain period of time, such as 10, 20, or 30 years, rather than the policyholder's entire life. If the policyholder dies during the time the policy is in effect—the term—the beneficiaries receive a payout. Term insurance premiums are generally lower than whole life insurance premiums.

If you don't have a family to support, there are better places to put your money. The only caution is that term life insurance policies tend to cost less the younger and healthier you are. But waiting until you're in your 20s or 30s won't mean a drastic increase in the premium.

Insurance salespeople may try to sell you an insurance policy that has cash value as a way to protect your family and as an investment. Don't bite. These policies are expensive, and it can be tough to find room in your budget for the monthly premiums. There are better tools for investing in your future. Plus many employers offer a term life insurance policy worth one to two times your annual salary as an employee benefit. That may be enough.

Disability insurance replaces a portion of your income if you can't work for a few weeks because of a temporary condition, or if you have a chronic illness that keeps you from earning money for a long period of time. Sometimes disability insurance is included as an employee benefit. Your employer may pay for part or all of a policy or offer it as a benefit you can pay for yourself. Insurance agents also sell disability insurance policies.

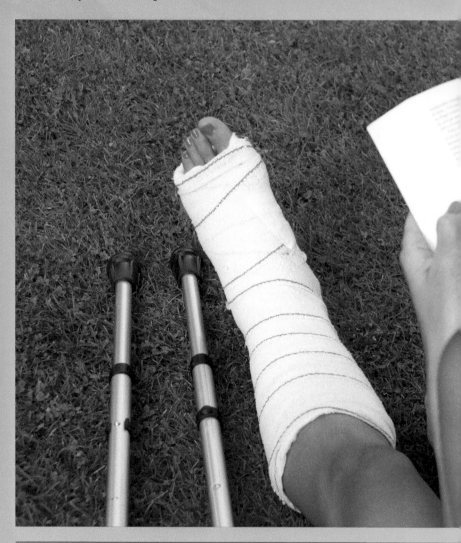

According to a survey by the online personal finance company Learnvest and Guardian Life Insurance Company, just 35 percent of 20- and 30-somethings have disability insurance of any kind. Most report that they don't know anyone who has become disabled or they don't think they need it for the kind of work that they do.

You might agree with the young adults who responded to the survey. You are young and healthy and don't need to scrape together money in your budget to buy insurance that covers you in the rare case that you become disabled. But it's more common for a young person to become disabled than you think. The U.S. Social Security Administration says that one in four of today's 20-year-olds will become disabled sometime during their careers.

Social Security offers disability insurance to workers who have paid into the system. But that usually isn't an adequate amount of coverage for workers and doesn't help in the event of a shorter-term illness or injury.

If your identity is stolen, it can take dozens of hours and a lot of hard work to clean up the mess. So how can you protect yourself from this crime? Nothing is foolproof, but following some simple precautions can greatly reduce your chance of becoming an identity theft victim.

- *Be careful about sharing sensitive information such as your Social Security number, your driver's license number, or your bank account number. Always ask why this information is necessary, and check with your parents or guardians if you have any doubt—even if it's a friend who is asking.*

- *Keep important documents safe. Never carry your birth certificate or Social Security card. Keep them in a locked safe at home or in a safe-deposit box at a bank.*

- *Shred, shred, shred. Never just throw away or recycle bank account statements or other papers with important numbers in plain sight. Shredding these documents and tossing the remnants in multiple recycling bins or garbage cans can thwart criminals.*

- *Check over your bank and credit card statements carefully. If someone else is using your account or credit card, you'll notice charges you don't recognize.*

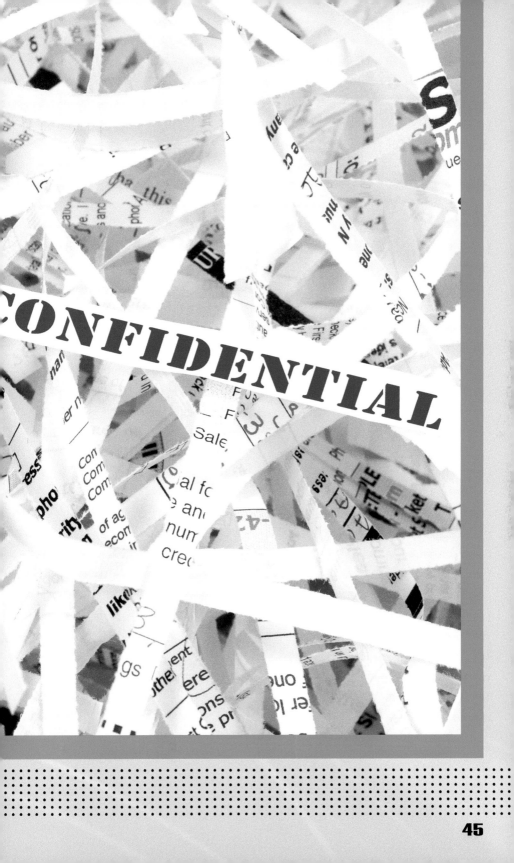

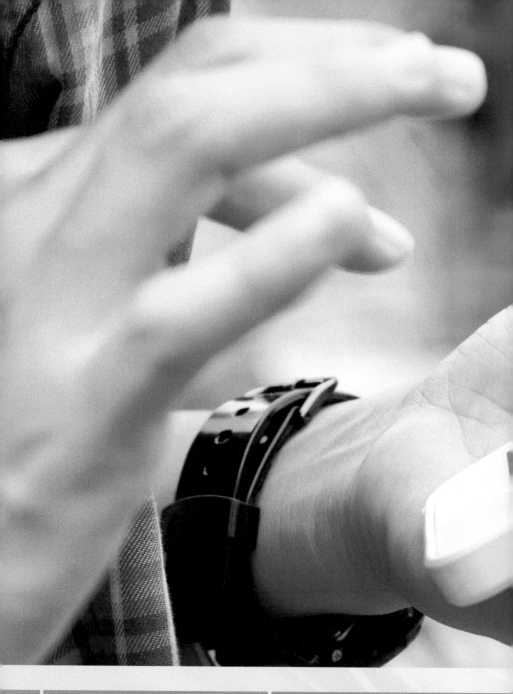

SIMPLE PRECAUTIONS

- Lock 'em up. Use the passcode function on your phone and the password feature on your laptop to protect your devices.

- Smartphones are a prime target for identity theft. You can reduce your risk by updating your operating system whenever the manufacturer makes an update available.

- Don't overshare. Keep personal info you share online to a minimum. For example, don't put your birth year, school, or middle name on your social media profiles. Also don't share any information online, such as your pet's name or grandparent's first name, that you may use as answers for security questions that helps verify your identity at a website.

- Check your credit report. Each year you are entitled to a free credit report from each of the three major credit bureaus from the website www.annualcreditreport.com. Access your report only through this official site. Other sites advertise free credit reports but often require other purchases to unlock your report. Steer clear. If you request one credit report every four months, it's a good way to monitor whether your identity has been stolen without having to pay for an identity theft monitoring service.

WHAT TO DO

Identity thieves can thwart even the most careful consumer. If you discover that your identity has been stolen, immediately take these steps to prevent further damage:

FRAUD ALERT

Place a fraud alert on your credit report. Find the number to call of one of the major credit reporting agencies—Equifax, Experian, or TransUnion—on their website.

FILE REPORT

File a police report.

CLOSE ACCOUNTS

Close any compromised accounts and dispute any charges that you didn't incur by contacting your credit card company, which will open up an investigation.

LODGE COMPLAINT

File a complaint with the Federal Trade Commission at https://www.ftccomplaintassistant.gov and create an identity theft report. It can be used to fight fraudulent charges and any other fallout from your stolen identity.

GOVERNMENT PROTECTION

Insurance, diligence, and reducing risky behaviors go a long way to protect you and your assets. But the government plays a role in protecting its citizens too. Many government agencies exist in part to make sure citizens aren't taken advantage of by corporations or financial institutions. They are resources if you have questions, problems, or complaints.

· ·

Attorney General: The attorney general is the chief legal officer of a state. One of the attorney general's primary jobs is to safeguard consumers from fraud or unfair business practices. In recent years attorneys general have gone after debt collection companies that haven't followed the law, utility companies that try to raise rates too high, and home security system companies that mislead senior citizens.

Consumer Financial Protection Bureau: The CFPB educates consumers about financial products, supervises banks and other financial companies, and enforces federal consumer finance laws. The bureau also collects consumer complaints, focusing its time and research on products that are particularly troubling to consumers. These include student loans, mortgages, and payment products such as credit cards and prepaid cards.

Federal Deposit Insurance Corporation: The FDIC was created after the Great Depression (1929–1939), when thousands of banks failed and many Americans lost their savings. The primary purpose of the FDIC is to insure up to $250,000 of a customer's deposits in the event that a bank goes out of business. The FDIC also examines and supervises banks to make sure they are operating properly and following laws designed to protect consumers.

The Franklin Delano Roosevelt Memorial in Washington, D.C., features sculptures of men in a Depression-era breadline.

The Federal Reserve building in Washington, D.C.

Federal Reserve: The Federal Reserve is the central bank of the United States. It establishes and sets up monetary policy, regulates and supervises banks, and operates the payment system. It also handles consumer complaints about banks and educates consumers about bank-related topics.

Federal Trade Commission: The FTC makes sure that businesses are not engaging in unfair or deceptive practices that put consumers at a disadvantage. The FTC educates consumers about money and business matters and informs them about common scams. The FTC is an excellent resource for learning about identity theft, your rights when you're in debt, and how to file a complaint with a company.

Securities and Exchange Commission: The SEC's primary job is to protect investors. It keeps tabs on financial planners to make sure they are following the laws designed to protect Americans' money. It also educates consumers about various markets available to invest in for retirement and other goals. The commission also makes sure that stock and bond markets run efficiently and fairly.

Experts suggest a different password for every account to avoid problems in case one of them experiences a security breach. Having to remember dozens of complex passwords is tough, especially since writing them down carries its own risks. But you don't want to be the chump who uses "password," "123456," or another easy-to-guess and all-too-common password to access your bank account.

Wondering how to create foolproof passwords that you can remember? Here are some suggestions:

Make it eight: Make your password at least eight characters long. A sentence might be easier to remember than a combination of random characters.

Mix it up: Create a password that includes several uppercase and lowercase letters, numbers, symbols, and punctuation marks.

Change it up: Don't keep the same passwords forever. Yes, it's a hassle to switch them, and most accounts don't require password resets. But experts recommend you set a reminder every three months to change your passwords.

After following these tips, if you still wonder how your password stacks up, run it through an online password checker, such as Microsoft Safety and Security Center, https://www.microsoft.com/security/pc-security/password-checker.aspx.

TIME IS MONEY

Resolving identity theft issues is time-consuming. According to Javelin Strategy and Research, identity theft victims spend about 58 hours trying to repair damage to their existing accounts and 165 hours fixing the damage caused by new accounts fraudulently opened in their names. That's the equivalent of more than five 40-hour work weeks!

KEEP IT SAFE

One of rapper Ice Cube's most famous songs pretty much sums up the concept of protection: "You better check yourself before you wreck yourself."

Being careful, taking calculated risks, sniffing out scams, and knowing when to say no are key skills in life and finance. You now know the basics of risk and how to determine your own risk tolerance. You can protect your belongings using insurance and knowing which types of insurance make sense for young adults and which can be skipped.

Finally, you are able to safeguard your most important assets—your earning potential, your identity, and your life. Protection is your financial foundation. Without it, you risk everything. You now have the tools to build a rock-solid financial life.

GLOSSARY

asset—item of value, such as money or property

attorney general—chief lawyer of a state or country

claim—request for payment of a loss covered by an insurance policy

commission—fee paid to an agent or employee for transacting a piece of business or performing a service

consumer—someone who buys and uses goods and services

deductible—amount of money an insured person pays before an insurance company pays for the remainder of the cost

escrow account—account, typically related to a home mortgage, where money is kept by a third person until it's time to pay insurance or other expenses

identity theft—stealing another person's identification and other personal information to use for financial gain

insurance score—rating computed and used by insurance companies that represents the probability that an insured person will file an insurance claim during his or her coverage

policy—written agreement for insurance between an insurance company and a person who has insurance

premium—amount paid for insurance

quote—amount of money that an insurance company calculates as the cost of providing insurance

warranty—written statement that promises the good condition of a product and states that the maker is responsible for repairing or replacing the product, usually for a certain period of time after its purchase

ADDITIONAL RESOURCES

FURTHER READING

Connolly, Sean. *Insurance*. Mankato, Minn.: Amicus, 2011.

Gagne, Tammy. *A Teen Guide to Protecting and Insuring Assets*. Hockessin, Del.: Mitchell Lane Publishers, 2014.

Hungelmann, Jack. *Insurance for Dummies*. Indianapolis: Wiley Pub. Inc., 2009.

Karchut, Wes, and Darby Karchut. *Money and Teens: Savvy Money Skills*. Colorado Springs, Colo.: Copper Square Studios, 2012.

INTERNET SITES

Use FactHound to find Internet sites related to this book. All of the sites on FactHound have been researched by our staff.

Here's all you do:

Visit *www.facthound.com*

Type in this code:
9780756549213

OTHER SITES TO EXPLORE

The Mint
http://www.themint.org

MyMoney.gov—Protect
http://www.mymoney.gov/protect/Pages/Protect.aspx

Teen Space—Protect Yourself
http://www.idtheftcenter.org/id-theft/teen-space.html

Benefitspro. 2 May 2014. http://www.benefitspro.com

Car Insurance Rates by State. Insure.com. 2 May 2014. http://www.insure.com/car-insurance/car-insurance-rates.html

Consumer Financial Protection Bureau. 2 May 2014. http://www.consumerfinance.gov

Consumers Union. 2 May 2014. http://consumersunion.org

Demystifying the Insurance Industry: The Truth About Insurance. 2 May 2014. http://www.thetruthaboutinsurance.com

Disability Planner: Social Security Protection If You Become Disabled. 2 May 2014. http://www.ssa.gov/dibplan/

Federal Trade Commission: Protecting America's Consumers. 2 May 2014. http://www.ftc.gov

HealthCare.gov. 2 May 2014. https://www.healthcare.gov

High School Financial Planning Program. 2 May 2014. http://www.hsfpp.org

Identity Theft Resource Center. 2 May 2014. http://www.idtheftcenter.org

Insurance Information Institute. 2 May 2014. http://www.iii.org

National Association of Insurance Commissioners. 2 May 2014. http://www.naic.org

National Crime Prevention Council. 2 May 2014. http://www.ncpc.org

INDEX

About the Author

Kara McGuire is an award-winning personal finance writer, consumer researcher, and speaker. She writes a personal finance column for the Minneapolis *Star Tribune* and formerly worked for the public radio program *Marketplace Money*. She enjoys teaching young people and parents about money. Kara lives in St. Paul, Minnesota, with her husband, Matt, and children Charlotte, Teddy, and August.